The Oatmeal Bath

and Other Poems that Make Kids Laugh

Lorraine L. Hollowell

Order this book online at www.trafford.com
or email orders@trafford.com

Most Trafford titles are also available at major online book retailers.

Printed in the United States of America.

ISBN: 978-1-4669-7926-0 (sc)
ISBN: 978-1-4669-7925-3 (e)

Trafford rev. 01/31/2013

 www.trafford.com

North America & international
toll-free: 1 888 232 4444 (USA & Canada)
phone: 250 383 6864 ◆ fax: 812 355 4082

This book is dedicated to my husband, James,
my daughter, Sharlene, my son, William "Bill,"
and all the children I've ever taught.

Table of Contents

Grandma June Wears Glasses

Grandma June wears glasses.
With them, she sees fine,
But without her two inch glasses on
Grandma's nearly blind.

Today she thought she was feeding
Little Nat in his high chair,
But it wasn't Little Nat at all.
It was Little Nat's teddy bear.

Once she walked into a tree
In Reverence Maxwell's yard.
Too bad she didn't see that tree
'Cause she bumped her head real hard.

When Reverend Maxwell came outside,
She thought he was a snake.
She hit him five times on his head
With his brand new wooden rake.

She lost her glasses at the park
And couldn't see a thing.
She caught a squirrel with a fishing rod
And barbequed a swing.

Yes, Grandma June wears glasses,
And with them, she sees swell.
Too bad she wasn't wearing them
When she fell down the well.

Lorraine L. Hollowell

Tackled Peanut Butter

My brother began to shake his head.
He shook it up and down.
He shook that head from side to side
And ferociously all around.

"Peanut butter's stuck up in my mouth,
And it won't come down.
What am I going to do?" he said,
With a halfway mumbled frown.

"I've tried and tried to get it free.
It's stuck up there like glue!
It refuses to release itself.
It's been there since half past two!"

I said, "Don't worry, Little Brother.
I'll get it down somehow.
Just open up your mouth real wide!
I'll get that stuff down now!"

"A sturdy kitchen spoon," I said
"Will surely do the trick."
But I was wrong; that peanut butter
Was determined it would stick.

Stick to my brother's mouth, that is!
It wasn't coming down.
So I reached for a butcher knife,
But my brother gave a frightened frown.

I put the butcher knife away
And picked up the spoon again.
I was more determined now
That the peanut butter wouldn't win.

Once more I took that kitchen spoon
And stuck it in his mouth.
It took me two hours to loosen it,
But I finally got it out.

Lorraine L. Hollowell

Save Me! I'm Hungry!

Mom fell in some quicksand
Yesterday afternoon.
She called me on her cell phone
And told me to bring a broom.

She said, "Please hurry, dear!
I'm feeling so much hunger.
I haven't had a bite all day
And I can't hold on much longer!

I'm sinking awfully fast, dear.
Hunger has made me weak.
Before this quicksand covers me
Please bring me a piece of meat!

You can use the broom to pull me out,
But pleeeasssse, let me eat first,
And along with the meat, bring lemonade
To satisfy my thirst."

I quickly rushed out of the house
With a broom in my right hand.
But after fifteen minutes,
Back to the house, I ran.

I'd forgotten the meat and lemonade.
Oh, how could I forget!
I couldn't arrive without them
'Cause Mom would be upset.

I got home in sixteen minutes
And made some lemonade.
It sure did taste delicious!
It was the best I'd ever made!

Next I opened up the frig
And removed a slice of ham,
Two slices of baloney,
And a left over piece of spam.

I dashed out of the house this time
With the lemonade and the meat.
Mom would be real proud of me
For bringing her this treat.

When I arrived, the quicksand
Had nearly reached Mom's chin.
She shouted, "I'll open my mouth wide.
Just toss the meat right in!"

Lorraine L. Hollowell

I tossed it directly into her mouth,
And she began to eat.
In less than seven seconds,
She'd eaten all the meat.

Then she said, "Go get the broom.
Put the lemonade at the end.
Then pass it slowly this way-
Right up to my chin."

I put the lemonade on the broom.
Then I passed it to my mom,
Before I could blink my eyes,
The lemonade was all gone.

On Mom's face was a big, big smile.
She liked my lemonade.
She said it was the best lemonade
That I had ever made.

Then quickly, she reached for the broom,
And I slowly pulled her out.
When she was freed from the quicksand,
Mom began to shout,

"Oh, thank you! Thank you!" she exclaimed.
"Without you, I'd be dead!
Come on! Let's hurry home now!
I want a piece of bread!"

Mom's Bad Luck

"Seven years of bad luck!"
Mom shouted from her room.
"Before I step on a piece of glass,
Someone, bring me the broom!

I broke a mirror; I'm in for it!
Glass is everywhere!
It's under the sofa, near the lamp,
And over there by the rocking chair.

There's glass on top of the TV stand;
And under the living room table.
I need to sweep this glass up now
While I'm still strong and able!

Bad luck is sure to come my way—
Seven years of it, in fact.
Please bring me the broom immediately,
Before I break my back!

And after I sweep this glass up,
I'm going straight to bed.
It's the safest place for me to go
To keep from dropping dead."

Kangarooapoo

Once there was a kangaroo
Who tried to leave its mother's poo.
Oh, no! I mean a kangarrouch
Who tried to leave its mother's pouch.

Oh, my, I think I've got it wrong.
I'm sure I sound like some dingdong.
However, he tried hard to escape
From his mother's kangerpape.

But whenever he tried to get away,
The tighter she closed her kangarpay.
Oh, will I ever get this right?
Was it kangaroo or kangarplight?

But eventually, he *did* get free
From his mother's kangarpee.
When she opened wide her
kangerpout,
The little kangeroo jumped out.

This poem was inspired by
Laura E. Richard's
"Eletelephony"

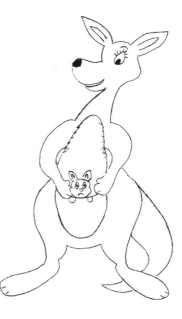

The Scent

I was camping in the Blue Ridge Mountains.
What a beautiful sight to see!
What a peaceful time I was having
Until a little skunk sprayed me.

The skunk came out of nowhere
While I was putting up my tent.
As soon as he set his eyes on me,
He let out the most horrible scent!

That scent went round about me.
It traveled up my nose,
And then that stinky, smelly scent
Penetrated my camping clothes.

I quickly took off everything
Down to my underwear.
Luckily, not a soul saw me.
I was the only one out there.

I washed my body in the lake,
But the scent wouldn't go away.
That stinky scent just lingered on.
It insisted it would stay!

For two whole days, I could smell that scent!
How I longed for it to flee!
I just couldn't stand being near myself
While that scent lingered on, on me.

Lorraine L. Hollowell

Danny Hugged a Porcupine

Danny hugged a porcupine,
And now he's full of holes.
I told him not to do it,
But this is what he chose:

He chose to hug the porcupine
That came wobbling in his yard.
I warned him not to touch it,
But Danny's head is hard.

He reached out to that porcupine
And hugged with all his might.
You should see poor Danny now!
He's such a holey sight!

There are needle holes all over him—
His arms, his legs, his face.
Wherever he's not wearing clothes,
You'll see holes in that place.

But Danny doesn't mind at all.
He says he's feeling fine,
And he's proud to be the only kid
Who's hugged a porcupine.

Where's the Turkey?

We were having roast turkey
For dinner that Sunday night.
Mom had stuffed it with cornbread dressing
And had seasoned it just right.

We could smell the fine aroma.
Oh, it smelled like it was yummy!
I could hardly wait to put
That tasty turkey in my tummy!

Along with ears of buttered corn,
Collard greens and sweet potatoes,
Carrots, cranberry sauce,
And my grandma's stewed tomatoes.

Yes, the turkey was in the oven,
But in ten minutes it would be done.
We'd waited hours for it to cook.
It must have weighed a ton!

The table was set and ready
When the timer went, "Ding, ding."
Mom opened the oven carefully.
But where was that tasty thing!?

Where on earth was the turkey!
We just didn't know.
But Mom had basted it in the oven
Just a little while ago.

It had disappeared—that turkey,
And only its bones were left,
So we came to the conclusion
That the turkey had eaten itself.

Lorraine L. Hollowell

Chocolate Fever

I came down with it
Late last night.
Just had to have a chocolate bite!

Chocolate fever
Had gotten the best of me.
I was running a temperature of a hundred and three.

My mouth was watering
For a chocolate bar.
To get one, I was willing to travel quite far—

To the moon,
Or even as far as the sun.
I'd go anywhere to get me one!

So I got out of bed,
And I looked all over,
Even on the back of my little dog, Rover.

When I discovered
I had eaten them all—
Not a bar in my house; none that I could recall,

I went next door
To my neighbor, McNair
To ask him if he had any chocolate to spare.

But he was out of chocolate
Just like me,
And like me, he had a temperature of a hundred and three.

Lorraine L. Hollowell

The Haircut

One day I sat upon a chair
As Dad began to cut my hair.
Too bad my dad was unaware
That I was going to sneeze.

Dad accidently shaved my top
Right down the middle in his barbershop.
There was no way I could make him stop
When I let out that sneeze.

Dad looked at me like he'd seen a bear.
Oh, what had he done to my beautiful hair?
Then Mom gave Dad an angry stare
After I let out that sneeze.

She shouted, "Honey, what have you done!?"
What have you done to my beautiful son!?"
Dad said, "Don't worry, I'll fix this one.
It's going to be a breeze."

Dad cut the rest of my hair away.
I ended up very bald that day—
So bald I refused to go out to play
For fear that I'd be teased.

But shortly to school, I had to go.
Guess what! My teacher loved my baldhead so
That she made me feel like a regular pro.
She made me feel at ease.

She asked, "May I call you *Little Shack?*
I think you look as sharp as a tack."
Don't worry if your hair never grows back!
Oh, keep it that way, please!!

She made me blush for a little while.
She made me feel like a handsome child,
And the kids seemed to like my new hair style.

You know . . .
I was kinda glad I sneezed.

Lorraine L. Hollowell

Grace

When my family sits down for dinner,
As my daddy says the grace,
My brother always looks at me
And makes a funny face.

My mommy has her head bowed.
The food, I can almost taste,
As my brother tries to make me laugh
With that silly, funny face!

Saved by Apple Pie

I was eating lunch in the jungle
When I heard a humming sound.
It was coming from behind me,
So I quickly turned around.

Just a few yards in front of me
Stood a funny-looking man.
He had a sharp knife in his mouth
And a spear in his right hand.

The moment I set my eyes on him,
I thought, "Who can he be?"
When he roared, I took off running,
And he ran right after me.

I ran as quickly as I could,
You should have seen me flee!
Then luckily, a thought came to me
To climb the nearest tree.

So up a tamarind tree I climbed
Until I reached the top,
But shortly, he was at the tree,
And he started looking up.

Lorraine L. Hollowell

I was shaking like a leaf up there.
Oh, what was I to do?
Then another thought came to me
To hit him with my shoe.

I threw not one, but two shoes down
Trying to hit his head.
But both shoes only hit the ground,
And he put them on instead.

I then thought sadly to myself,
"Today I just might die,
But if I must, first I'll eat
A slice of apple pie."

So, I reached inside my lunchbox,
And took out the slice of pie.
It's a good thing that I dropped it,
And here's the reason why:

It landed right inside his mouth,
And he ate that slice of pie.
Then he waved at me and walked away
Saying "Thank you" and "Good-bye."

How Can I Eat this Baked Potato?

How can I eat this baked potato
While its eyes look up at me?
Maybe I should blindfold it
To make sure it doesn't see.

Though it has a delicious body
So sour creamed and buttery,
It's just so hard for me to eat it
While its eyes look up at me.

Lorraine L. Hollowell

Don't Eat Me!

I tried to bite an apple
But much to my surprise,
It wouldn't let me bite it.
It looked me in the eyes
And said,
"Put me down this instant!
Don't make me your fruity food!
Go eat a pear or banana!
I'm just not in the mood!"

Picking on My Sister

I pick on my sister every chance I get.
When I read her diary or pull her hair,
She gets so upset!

I've put spiders in her pockets and lizards in her hat.
Today I found a dead black snake.
I'm gonna chase her around with that.

Yes, I pick on my sister; I've become her greatest foe!
But I won't let others pick on her
Because I love her so.

Lorraine L. Hollowell

Behave!

Don't lean back in your chair!
Do you want to fall?
Stop bouncing that thing in this house!
Please, put down that ball!

Get your elbows off the table!
Close your mouth when you eat!
Pick your clothes up off the floor!
Please, keep this bedroom neat!

Have you washed your hands today?
I doubt it! Look at that dirt!
Why are you playing with those matches!
Look out! Don't burn your shirt!

Take those skates off at once!
There's no skating in the house!
Haven't I told you a million times
Not to chase me with that mouse!

Are you drawing on the wall again!
Put those crayons away!
Stop jumping up and down on the bed!
Go outside and play!!

You're acting so irresponsible.
This for sure is true.
But you still mean the world to me,
And I'm glad I married you.

Lorraine L. Hollowell

Tag

Are you bored?
Are you idle?
Have nothing to do?
Do you think that life is a drag?
If you feel this way, my friend, today,
You know you can always play tag.

You can tag the floor, the wall, and the door.
You can tag the toilet stool too.
You can tag the rugs, all spiders and bugs.
You can even try tagging beef stew.

You'll never get bored tagging about.
It keeps one busy, you see?
But if you'd prefer not tagging these things.
Come on and try to tag me.

The Snake and the Mole

"Will you crawl into my hole?"
Said the snake to the mole.
"It's the most gorgeous little hole
That you'll ever behold!

Inside my little hole
Are things you'd love to eat.
Won't you come into my hole?
Please come down and have a treat!"

"Oh, no, no!" said the little mole,
"Your hole? No way! Not I!
I've learned my lesson
From the tale of
The Spider and the Fly.

This poem was inspired by "*The Spider and the Fly*"
written by Mary Howitt in 1829.

　　　　　Lorraine L. Hollowell

Just Plain Lazy

I was sent to the farm
Of Auntie Bess and Uncle Tom.
He milked the cows inside the barn.
She gathered eggs in the early morn.
But me?
I was just plain lazy.

My uncle fed the pigs and sheep.
My aunt, so clean, the house she'd keep.
He faithfully plowed the dusty fields,
And she cooked such delicious meals!
But me?
I was just plain lazy.

Then one day Uncle Tom looked at me
And asked, "Boy, why you so lazy?!
To live with us, you gotta do your share.
So get up off that rocking chair!
And stop that being lazy!"

And Auntie Bess said, "This ain't no hotel, son!
You weren't sent here to rip and run.
You were sent to work
And not have fun!
So stop that being lazy!"

I'm no longer on the farm
Of Auntie Bess and Uncle Tom.
In less than one week, I was gone
Cause me?
I'm just plain lazy.

A Creature Took It

Something landed on my roof
With half a body, and that's the truth.
It had one ear and a single eye.
Please believe me 'cause it's no lie.

The creature landed in a booth.
I saw it land upon my roof.
It came out and politely said,
"Gimme, gimme, gimme peg."

Lorraine L. Hollowell

With its half body, it hopped down.
It came down quickly to the ground.
It hopped to me on its one leg
Shouting, "Gimme, gimme, gimme peg!"

I had my homework in my hand.
It quickly grabbed it; then it ran.
Teacher, believe me 'cause it's a fact.
It refused to give my homework back.

I saw it hop back on the roof.
I saw it get back in its booth.
I saw the booth head for the sky.
And with my homework, it went bye-bye.

My Conscience is a Naughty Boy

My conscience is a naughty boy.
He's as bad as he can be!
I tell him to behave himself,
But will he listen to me?

Well, sometimes he *does* listen,
But often, he does not.
Today that boy was really bad!
Yes, he was bad a lot!

He told me to skip breakfast,
And on the bus, not to sit down.
And while my teacher was teaching,
He said, "Act like a clown."

I told him I should do my chores.
He told me I should play.
Because of him, I didn't do
One single chore today.

Yes, my conscience is a naughty boy-
As bad as he can be,
But I have faith one day he'll be
Just as good as me.

A Fly is in the Pie

Once I saw a little fly
Crawl into a slice pie—
Some juicy, yummy raisin pie
Belonging to my brother.

I saw my brother reach for it.
I saw him bite a tiny bit—
A very tiny little bit,
And then he bit another.

Next he bit a bigger bite.
He bit this bite with all his might.
This time he took a real big bite
Before he bit another.

He then continued biting on.
He bit until the slice was gone.
Not only the slice, but the fly was gone!
It was eaten by my brother!

I wanted to tell him about that fly-
The fly inside his slice of pie.
But I couldn't tell him; here's the reason why:
I'm just an infant brother.

Melvin is Like a Turtle

Melvin is like a turtle.
He creeps just like a snail.
Again and again he gets to school
After the tardy bell.
"Hurry up!" his mother says each day.
"You're going to miss the bus!"
"Oh, it's okay," he answers back.
"There's no need to rush."
Slowly, Melvin ties his shoes.
Much slower, he buttons his coat,
While his mother sits at the table
Writing his teacher a note.
It says:

Dear Mrs. Price,

I'd like for you to know
That when Melvin got out of bed
He was extremely slow!
I told him to speed things up,
But he wouldn't listen to me.
The more I insisted he hurry along,
The slower he moved, you see?"
It took him over an hour to eat
Only a slice of bread.
Then after eating his breakfast,
He went straight back to bed.
So this is why he's tardy again.
But I won't be his fool.
I've come up with the solution.
Let him reside at school!

Sincerely,
Melvin's Mom

Lorraine L. Hollowell

A Passing Grade!

I've finally made a passing grade!
I knew that I could do it.
I knew that if I'd do my best
There would be nothing to it.

I listened as my teacher taught.
She couldn't believe her eyes.
I focused so attentively
That it took her by surprise!

She thought I was a new kid
When she saw me look her way.
She asked, "Where did you come from?"
And "Are you here to stay?"

I said, "Of course I am, Miss Ach.
I'm your student, Georgie Grange.
From now on I will do my best.
I'm gonna make a change.

With two more days left in this year,
Somehow I'm gonna make it.
But if I can't keep this behavior up,
Then maybe I can fake it."

Always a Teacher

My mother is a teacher
With a class of twenty-three.
Even in the evenings,
She's never "teacher free."

We have a chalkboard in our home
And hall passes with *B* and *G*.
Mom's just a regular teacher.
She can't give it up, you see?

I think she's been this way for years—
Since receiving her degree.
Why would she want to teach twenty-three kids
And then teach my sister and me?

Whenever I'm doing my homework,
Mom says, "Keep that paper neat!"
When I get up to get water, she says,
"Go back and take your seat!"

Mom even calls the roll at home.
She double-checks it too.
If my sister or I would ever skip class,
There's no telling what Mom would do!

Lorraine L. Hollowell

Are We Moving to the Mountains?

Dad, are we moving to the mountains?
I don't want to live up high!
I'd rather live in a valley
Than way up high, up near the sky.

I might trip at the very top, Dad.
I might fall down on the ground.
Suppose I bump into a tree or two
As I continue rolling down?

Wild animals live in the mountains, Dad!
I might run into a bear!
What will I do if he comes charging?
Dad, I don't want to live up there!

Are we moving to the mountains?
Are we really moving up?
Tell me, Dad, please tell me!

Well, Son . . .
The answer's "Yep."

The Junkyard

I love going to the junkyard,
But I know I should stay away.
If my parents ever caught me playing there,
I'd be grounded for at least a day.
The junkyard is the place to go,
If you're looking for some fun.
There are really neat things to find out there
And several places to rip and run!

Once I found an old beat up chest
While running up a hill.
When I took it home, Mom shouted,
"That thing might make us ill!"
I found a rocking chair there once
That I thought Dad would adore,
But when he saw it, he yelled out loud,
"What'd you bring that thing here for?!"

I try to stay away from it,
But I pass it every day.
I have to walk to school, you know?
And the junkyard's on the way.
Last week I found an old black comb
That I gave to Miss McClean.
When I told her where it came from,
All she could do was scream.

I guess it's just those grown-ups
That don't like junkyard things.
'Cause my friends . . . well, we all love 'em,
And the fun the junkyard brings.

Lorraine L. Hollowell

Cousin Brig Almost Drowned

Cousin Brig drank so much water
That she almost drowned.
Aunt Swanee called the rescue squad,
And here's what the medics found:

Brig drank at least thirty gallons—
Maybe more in just one day.
We don't know why she did it.
The medics didn't say.

But, they *did* say they'd have to pump it out
For my cousin to survive.
Aunt Swanee said, "Go right ahead.
I want my girl alive!"

They pumped, and pumped, and pumped some more
Until they'd pumped enough,
And Brig survived that wet ordeal.
Heavens! That girl is tough!

Eight glasses a day is her limit now.
She won't drink another drop,
And Aunt Swanee's so very proud of her
'Cause she now knows when to stop.

Lorraine L. Hollowell

The Fixing Man

Some call Joe *Mr. Fixing*
Others call him *The Fixing Man*.
If something breaks in your house,
Joe can fix it; yes, he can!

Your refrigerator's not working?
Your freezer's conked out too?
No problem because *The Fixing Man*
Can fix them both for you.

He'll have them working in no time.
They'll be as good as new.
And Joe won't charge an arm or leg
The way some others do.

He can fix clogged drains and TV sets,
Tables and broken chairs,
Stoves that give no heat,
And fans that give no air.

Don't buy new furniture or appliances.
Mr. Fixing can save you cash.
And he won't take forever,
He can fix things in a flash!

Once Joe fixed a toenail,
He glued it back on me!
This proves that he's a *fixing* man.
He's the best! I guarantee!

Lorraine L. Hollowell

Bumped Toe

Oh, no! Oh, no!
I bumped my toe!
My big fat toe!
And it hurts so!

If Mom were here,
She'd kiss my toe
Just like she did
Forty years ago.

My Funny Bones Started Laughing

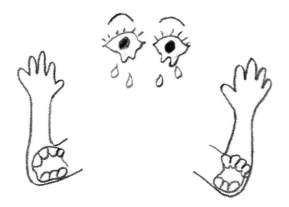

My funny bones started laughing
When they witnessed what I did,
But my eyes said, "My!" and began to cry
When they saw me bump my head.

Lorraine L. Hollowell

Real Sinclair

Mothers and daughters, please listen.
Fathers and sons, bewave.
Old and young, take my advice,
If you want to keep your hair.

There's a shampoo on the market.
It's called *Real Sinclair*,
But the only thing it really does
Is take away your hair.

I used it on my daughter
And on my sister, Pat.
Now my daughter wears a wig,
And Pat always wears a hat.

Real Sinclair removed their hair.
They're as bald as they can be.
Neither has a bit of hair
For anyone to see.

So mothers and daughters, please listen.
Fathers and sons, bewave.
Young and old, take my advice:
Don't shampoo with *Real Sinclair*!

Aunt Sue Went Bowling

The other day Aunt Sue went bowling.
She threw the ball, and it went rolling,
And Aunt Sue went rolling too.

They both went rolling down the aisle,
And straight ahead there was a pile
Of bowling pins, so new.

Then . . .

STRIKE!

Everyone clapped for my Aunt Sue,
And everyone clapped for the bowling ball too.
Together they knocked down every pin, so new—
The bowling ball and my dear Aunt Sue!

Lorraine L. Hollowell

Invisible Letters

I looked in my mailbox,
And what did I see?
An invisible letter
Addressed only to me.

I opened it up
And to my surprise
It said absolutely nothing
Before both my eyes.

Now, these kinds of letters
Are extremely rare.
I longed to share it!
But it just wasn't there.

It wasn't written
In pencil or ink,
Or on paper that's yellow,
White, blue or pink.

It wasn't in cursive,
Nor was it in print.
It didn't give the date,
Or from whom it was sent.

But I decided
To answer back anyway,
And an invisible letter,
I wrote the very same day.

Bad Aim

We were playing ball at Deer Park
With two hours to go before it got dark.

I hit the ball above a lake
Near the Mariners' Museum by mistake.

When the ball dropped down into the lake,
It was caught instantly by a water snake.

Inside his mouth, he caught that ball.
He didn't let it drop at all.

He tried to throw it back to me,
But his aim was poor, and it hit a tree.

Off the tree, it bounced; then it hit Ted.
It hit poor Ted right on his head.

Lorraine L. Hollowell

Then off Ted's head and into the lake,
And again it was caught by the water snake.

This time the snake aimed it at Jack,
But instead, it hit Mike on his back.

It bounced once more into the lake.
Who was there to catch it? The water snake!

He threw it quickly up in the air.
It landed, but, we know not where.

But here's what we *do* know about that ball:
That snake can't throw it straight at all!

My Neighbor, the Cat

I'm certain my neighbor
Was once a cat
With nine long lives!
Imagine that!

Four times he almost
Drowned at sea.
Two times he drank
Some poisoned tea.

He lived after being
In a deadly plane crash.
Was run over by a truck,
But he wasn't mashed.

But last week in the forest
He was unaware
That he was being followed
By a hungry, black bear.

It attacked my neighbor
From behind,
And that black bear
Was far from kind!

It devoured my neighbor
Just like that.
It was the ninth and final life
Of my neighbor, the cat!

Lorraine L. Hollowell

The Runny Nose Race

Nathaniel had a runny nose.
It ran right off his face.
It rushed itself to Noseville
And entered the *Runny Nose Race*.

His nose was not a bit surprised
To see so many friends.
Sharlene's nose had entered the race
And so had Mike's and Glen's.

William's nose was also there.
So were Grant's and Tom's.
Erikka's, Bess's, and Pattie's too
And so was Pattie's mom's.

Along with these were twenty more
All runny and eager to go.
And as they neared the starting line,
They all began to blow.

When the flag went down, the noses ran,
And as they ran, they blew.
Tim's nose was in the front,
While Nathaniel's was number two.

Glen's nose was running fast—
Moving close in on Pattie's
His runny nose was in fourth place,
And in fifth place was Hattie's.

In last place was Purnell's nose,
But it was still determined.
In only a very little while,
It had caught up with Herman's.

Nathaniel's nose was easing up
Behind the nose of Tim.
And when his nose passed his friend, Tim,
He gave a wave at him.

The noses ran; the noses blew—
Each one at a steady pace.
But Nathaniel's nose ran fastest,
And it won the *Runny Nose Race*.

Lorraine L. Hollowell

Jason Steps on His Toes

Whenever Jason walks and wherever he goes,
He's constantly stepping on his own toes.

"Ouch, ouch!" you'll hear him say
Many times throughout the day.

He tries hard to stay off of them.
But his feet continue to step on him.

What causes him to do this, no one knows,
But I sure feel sorry for Jason's toes!

Feet, You Stink!

"Feet, you stink!"
Said its toes one day,
"And if you don't wash soon,
We're running away!"

A Tennis Shoe Nightmare

Last night I dreamt I was a shoe,
But not just any shoe.
I was the worn-out tennis shoe
Of Clifford T. Poopoo.

If you've ever seen this shoe;
If you've smelled it too,
Then you know it wasn't just a dream,
But a nightmare I went through!

Good-bye Nails

I bite my nails
When I take a test.
When I study well
I bite them less.

I've not studied my best
In at least a year.
I must blame myself
If they disappear.

Hopping to the Wedding

I was traveling to Connecticut
When I fell out of a plane.
How fortunate I was
To have landed on a train!

It was traveling to Connecticut
At such tremendous speed . . .
So fast I knew I'd be in time
To see my aunt married.

But on the track was a fallen tree
Which caused the train to stop.
So, I got out very quickly
And began to pogo hop.

Since I'm the fastest pogo hopper
This world has ever known,
I can out hop anybody,
Both the young and fully-grown,

Whenever I go out of town,
I take my pogo stick with me.
And on this very special day
It came in so handy!

I hopped over roads and highways
And over bridges too.
Apartments, I hopped over
And even half a zoo.

When I had less than ten miles to go
Which wasn't very far,
I hopped over a bus, a moving van,
And then a speeding hybrid car.

I continued hopping on real fast,
As fast as I could hop.
There was nothing in this whole wide world
That would make my hopping stop.

I knew that I was very near
When I heard the church bell chime.
A few more hops, and I was there.
I'd made it just in time!

I was there when my aunt and her dad walked in.
I was there when she said, "I do."
I was there when the groom kiss his lovely bride,
And I threw rice at them too.

Yes, I made it to the wedding.
I sure did get there quick!
The plane and train may have let me down,
But not my pogo stick!

Lorraine L. Hollowell

Rocker's Locker

We were told to clean our lockers out—
To remove all junk inside.
You wouldn't believe what fell on the floor
When Rocker opened his wide!

On the floor fell some sweat pants—
Five, to be exact.
They had the most disgusting smell!
Believe me; it's a fact!

Two slices of bread were on one pair—
Each slice, about two-months-old.
I know because on top of each
Was a brownish-looking mold.

When a teddy bear fell on the floor,
Rocker tried to hide it quick.
He covered it with something red.
I think it was a brick.

A baseball bat, a radio,
And seven DVD's,
Six pairs of socks, two pairs of jeans,
And a can of black eyed peas.

An old telephone, a telephone book,
And a TV guide, as well,
About eight screws, an extension cord,
And an old grey rusty nail.

There was crumbled-up paper,
An old notebook and a deflated basketball.
A lot more junk fell on the floor,
But I just can't name it all.

Blinded by *Close Tight Glue*

I thought it was eye drop,
But it was *Close Tight Glue*.
It closed my eyes completely.
Oh, what was I to do?

I fumbled from the bathroom
And finally reached the den.
I had to call my doctor.
What a bad shape I was in!

I bumped into a table
And the TV set, as well.
And when I bumped into a chair,
It was then that I almost fell.

At last I found the telephone,
And I called Dr. Hue.
I thought I'd never reach him.
Calling blind was hard to do!

Lorraine L. Hollowell

I told him about the accident—
That my eyes were closed real tight.
I told him I'd tried to open them—
That I'd tried with all my might.

I begged, "Can you please help me?
I've made a big mistake!"
He replied, "No need to worry, dear.
There's something you can take.

It's *Close Tight Glue Remover,*
And it's a cinch to make."
He assured me it would take away
Any *Close Tight Glue* mistake.

He said, "You'll need a cup of vinegar,
And sugar, you'll need two,
A pint of vanilla, a quart of milk,
And a pinch of salt will do.

Just mix these things together;
Then quickly drink the drink.
The *Close Tight Glue* will soon dissolve,
And your eyes will start to blink."

Then those eyes of yours will open wide,
And they'll be as good as new."
I replied, "Well, that sounds simple.
Why, thank you, Doctor Hue."

In a little over an hour
The cure was in front of me.
I drank it very quickly.
It worked, and now I see!

Blue-Haired Sister

My sister's wearing blue underwear,
A blue sweater and blue dress.
Blue's the only color she ever wears
'Cause she likes blue the best.

Whenever she goes out to play,
The kids all stop and stare.
She wouldn't look so ridiculous
If she didn't have blue hair.

They point at her and call her names,
But she seems not to care
When they all shout, "Look, there she is!
The girl with the long blue hair!"

Lorraine L. Hollowell

My Sister and I are Opposites

My sister plays with baby dolls.
Not me! I play with frogs.
She likes to walk in Mom's high-heels.
I like to walk on logs.

My sister wears my mom's makeup.
I think she's much too young.
I'll never, ever understand
How she finds makeup fun.

I like climbing trees in our yard.
She likes to make mud pies.
I have no fear of wiggly snakes.
But, she's afraid of flies!!

The other day, she had the nerve
To ask me to play *House*.
I gave that girl one mean, hard look
Then chased her with a mouse.

I'm sure she won't ask me again.
She's learned her lesson well.
I'll never play that sissy stuff!
I'd rather go to jail!

Yes, my sister and I are opposites;
We're as opposite as can be,
But, I love my sister very much,
And I'm pretty sure she loves me.

Lorraine L. Hollowell

Won Day I'll Bee a Mathematishon

I'm a prettie good speler, as you kan sea,
But math is relly my cup of tee!

Won day I'll bee a mathematishon.
That's my goal—my numbir won misshon.

My frends all say that I'm just wishin.
Thay say I'll never bee a mathematishon!

But, I love numbirs! Yes siree!
My favorit numbirs are 1,2,3.
I like two add them up, you sea?
And a mathematishon is what I'll be!

2+3 is 12, I'm sure.
And 13 + 3 is 24.
12+3 is always 8,
And 3+12 is 10,
But wait . . .

I kan add larger numbirs two.
Wach and sea what I kan do:
83+90 is 102.

Yes, I'm a prettie good speler, as you kan sea,
But math is relly my cup of tee!

Mom's Ironing

We can't trust Mom's ironing
Because she often burns our clothes.
Just the other day, she burned
Her no-tear panty hose.

She burned Dad's only handkerchief
And then Dad's brand new shirt.
But that's not all; on that same day,
Mom burned my favorite skirt!

There are holes in my brother's pajamas.
Bigger holes are in his pants.
Since Mom burned my sister's new dress,
She's skipping this year's *Ring Dance!*

Mom loves to iron, but we wish she'd stop.
She's ruining so many clothes!
If she doesn't quit her ironing soon,
All our clothes will have holes.

Lorraine L. Hollowell

No Homework

Teacher, I didn't do my homework
'Cause our lights went out last night,
And when Dad finally got them on
My pencil wouldn't write.

The lead just kept on breaking
And the pencil sharpener, too.
Nothing was working properly,
So what was I to do?

No, I didn't do my homework
'Cause our lights went out last night.
Of course, if I'd had done it,
All my answers would be right.

Miss Dercy

Miss Dercy is so nice to us
Whenever we are good.
She often bribes us with rewards
Like every teacher should.

When we walk quietly down the hall,
She gives us little treats,
Like jelly beans and lollipops,
Or other kinds of sweets.

However, when we misbehave,
Miss Dercy gets so mean!
She becomes the meanest teacher
That I have ever seen!

Lorraine L. Hollowell

If we walk down the hall
Making even the slightness sound,
That beautiful, friendly smile of hers
Becomes an evil frown.

We must never interrupt her
While she's teaching something new,
And we mustn't argue with her.
If we do, then we are through!

We mustn't lie, cheat, or steal,
Or vandalize our desks.
If we attempt to do these things,
We'll be in one big mess!

All homework must be turned in.
We can't be late for school.
We must obey Miss Dersey
And *never* break a rule!

If we decide to break a rule,
It sure upsets Miss Dersey.
And when Miss Dersey gets upset,
Miss Dersey shows no mercy.

My Teacher's Like a Tornado

My teacher's like a tornado.
She won't slow down one bit!
She's always running about the room.
I've never seen her sit!

From the front of the room to the back of the room,
She moves from child to child.
Sometimes I think my teacher is
Just plain old teaching wild!

She'll say, "Does anyone need my help?
Does everyone understand?
If there's anything you need help with,
Then kids, just raise your hand."

She moves quickly from corner to corner
And quickly from side to side,
Looking over all our shoulders,
But sometimes . . . I wish she'd hide!

Lorraine L. Hollowell

The Mosquito

A mosquito was in my room last night.
It wouldn't let me be.
It kept on buzzing in my ear.
It kept disturbing me.

I tried to shoo that thing away,
But it refused to go.
Then suddenly I got an itch
Upon my big fat toe.

My shoulder started itching, too—
The shoulder on my right.
That little, tiny monster
Had gotten another bite.

I then crawled under my blankets.
I was covered from head to toe,
But this didn't do the trick at all.
It continued to bite me so!

It bit me through those blankets—
Two blankets and one sheet.
It aimed at me very carefully.
It bit my rump and feet.

I finally decided I'd had enough,
And I turned on the light.
When I spotted it sitting on my bed,
I swung with all my might!

I tried to hit it with my hand,
But it was too quick for me.
And then that little monster
Managed to bite my knee.

It then flew to my pillow
Where I hit it with a whack,
But just before I clobbered it,
There was an itch upon back.

Yes, I managed to hit that monster.
That mosquito was surely done!
And I felt so very good inside
'Til I spotted another one.

Lorraine L. Hollowell

The Black Cat

I was walking through the woods on a dark, lonely path
When I saw a black cat, and I heard him laugh.
He said, "I'm going home with you to kill *that* rat."
I said, "What rat?!" and "I don't need a cat!"

Then I turned around and went the other way,
But he followed me home and decided he'd stay.
When he moved in with me . . . inside my house,
He not only caught a rat, but a little grey mouse!

That black cat brought me good luck, not bad.
And I'm so glad he lives with me in my pad.
He's shown me superstitious stuff doesn't matter.
But I'm still not walking under any latter.

Don't Signs

There's a story I'd like to tell.
I've learned my lesson and learned it well.
Please listen to me; this story is free . . .

From now on, I'll obey every sign,
Especially, those that say, "Don't."
"Don't exceed the speed limit,"
"Don't litter,"
"Don't pass,"
"Don't open the door,"
"Don't step on the grass,"
"Don't enter here,"
"Don't hit the hay,"
If the sign says, "Don't," I'll obey.

Last summer I saw a sign at the Woo Loo Zoo—
A sign that said, "Don't feed the kangaroo."
But I thought to myself, "What would a little nut do?"
So I reached in my pocket and threw the kangaroo two.

Lorraine L. Hollowell

Suddenly, he got a hold of his cage
And pulled two bars apart in a terrible rage.
Then he hopped right out of his kangaroo cage
In that horrible, terrible kangaroo rage!

I took off running as fast as a flash.
He charged at me as quick as a dash.
In the process, I think I developed a rash,
As I thought to myself, "I'm going to be hash!"

He caught up with me and grabbed me real tight.
Then he put up his fist; he wanted to fight!
So I grabbed his right leg, and I gave it a bite.
I bit his right leg with all of my might.
Then I bit and I bit
And I bit it some more.
I knew that his right leg
Had to be sore!

He tried to hit me
As he swung with his fist.
He tried and he tried,
But he missed and he missed.

And I bit him some more
'Til he gave up the fight.
Then he hopped back to his cage,
But . . . he was alright.

Me?
I was shaking . . .
I had no idea
How frightened I was!
How filled up with fear . . .

Until the kangaroo
Was back in his cage.
It was then that I fainted
Due to kangaroo rage.

This story to you,
I just had to tell.
I've learned my lesson,
And I've learned it well . . .
If the sign says, "Don't," then I won't!

Please listen to me; this advice is free:
If the sign says "Don't," then just don't!

Lorraine L. Hollowell

My Dad's a Bona Fide Rock Hound

My dad's a bona fide rock hound.
He's *forever* collecting rocks!
There are rocks all over our living room floor
And rocks inside Dad's socks.

Dad cleans the rocks very carefully
When he brings them home at night.
He knocks off every bit of dirt
'Cause he wants them to shine bright.

There are rocks scattered under every bed,
Even some in our kitchen sink.
I suppose it could be a whole lot worse.
At least his rocks don't stink!

Chased by a Gorilla

It was three o'clock in the morning,
But I wasn't asleep in bed
'Cause I was running from a gorilla
With a monkey on his head.

He chased me around the living room,
In three bedrooms, and the den,
Around the kitchen, two times,
Then back and forth again.

He chased me up and down the stairs,
Then in and out the door.
Five times, we ran around my house,
Then straight to the grocery store.

Lorraine L. Hollowell

Into the grocery store, we ran,
Then up and down the aisles.
It seems to me that we had run
For miles and miles and miles.

He would not stop; I would not stop.
So, on and on we ran,
Until he finally caught up with me
And grabbed me by the hand.

He said, "I think we've run enough.
My monkey thinks so too.
We've got to stop this running now
And head back to the zoo."

Chased by a Pit Bull

When I was about eight months past three
In my backyard playing happily,
Tim, a pit bull, started chasing me,
But I ran faster than him.

How a young, little girl eight months past three
Can run so fast is a mystery!
That mean old pit bull couldn't catch me.
No way would he bite my limb!

I ran and ran as fast as I could.
He ran after me like any pit bull would.
My mother came out screaming like a mother should,
And her screaming frightened him.

Tim took off running . . . Yes siree!
He ran smack dab into a tree.
Never again has Tim messed with me
Since the day I outran him!

Lorraine L. Hollowell

Road Kill

If you're traveling along a highway,
And you spot road kill up ahead—
A squirrel, a deer, a rat, or cat,
Or something else that's dead,

Quickly pinch your nose real tight
And keep it pinched a while.
Take my advice and keep it pinched
For at least a mile.

Cold House

Last month, Dad was pretty shocked
When he got the electric bill.
"This month," he said, "embrace yourselves
And get ready for a little chill."

But this isn't just a little chill!
No, that can't be so!
I keep looking up at the ceiling
Expecting it to snow.

I'm wearing a pair of long johns,
Some gloves and an old wool hat,
Four pairs of socks, two pairs of pants,
And three shirts! Imagine that!

Lorraine L. Hollowell

The kitchen's like the North Pole,
My bedroom's like Pluto,
And when I use the bathroom,
I freeze from head to toe.

It's freezing in the living room,
But it's colder in the den.
From room to room, all over this house,
It's the coldest it's ever been!

Darrick was Never Bad Until . . .

Darrick Payne was never bad
Until Miss Costa made him mad.

He asked if he could lead the line.
She said, "Okay," then changed her mind.

She then said, "*Peter* will lead the line.
He turned his project in on time."

That made Darrick very mad.
He showed his teacher he could be bad!

He threw a pencil in the air
That landed in Miss Costa's hair.

Lorraine L. Hollowell

He said, "What a shame! My pencil slipped!"
Then instantly, he did a flip.

He threw his math book on the floor.
He kicked his desk and ran out the door.

He turned around and ran back in.
Then he ran back out and in again.

"Darrick!" Miss Costa said,
"Why on earth are you acting bad?

I've never seen *you* act this way!
What's the matter with you today?

What has gotten into you?
What's making you do these things you do?"

He said, "Miss Costa, *you* made me mad.
You're the reason I'm acting bad!

You said that *I* could be line leader,
But then, you gave the job to Peter.

Miss Costa, that just wasn't fair!
That's why there's a pencil in your hair."

She said, "You're right, and here's what I'll do.
I'm giving that job right back to you,

And I promise you, Darrick, that I'll be fair.
Just don't throw pencils in my hair."

If I Were Principal

If I were principal
Of a primary school
I'd get rid of most restrictions—
Almost every single rule!

I'd let the kids chew bubblegum
And blow and pop it too.
If there's something else they could do with it,
Then, that's something I'd let them do.

There would be no teachers lecturing.
None to say, "Please pay attention!"
None to tell the kids to sit up straight.
That causes so much tension!

Lorraine L. Hollowell

Notes would not be taken.
There'd be nothing to learn that's new.
And why bother with old learning?
'Cause they'd have nothing to review.

The kids would run from class to class
And skateboard down the hall.
I'd let them dance in the library
And draw pictures on the wall.

No need for those hall passes!
They're such a waste of time!
No need to ask to leave the room.
Just leaving would be fine.

From eight to nine, they'd watch TV.
From nine to ten, they'd play.
The kids would all be so content
That they'd never disobey!

From ten to eleven, they'd play some more,
From eleven to twelve o'clock too.
After all, playing's great exercise,
And it's what they'd rather do.

At twelve o'clock, they'd all eat lunch.
No sugarless or low fat stuff,
But ice cream, cake, and chocolate bars
Until they've had enough.

After lunch . . . I'm sure you've guessed.
I'd let them play some more.
I'm certain they wouldn't object one bit,
If I let them play 'til four.

There'd be no homework assignments,
No projects or studying for tests.
At home, the kids would have quality time
Playing games that they like the best.

With absolutely no homework—
No reading, no writing, no math,
They'd also have tons of TV time,
Watching shows that make them all laugh.

Being a principal can be hard work,
I've heard some people say,
But not for me . . . I'd watch TV
And join the kids at play.

Lorraine L. Hollowell

The Principal's Coming!

The principal's coming, boys and girls!
Everyone, sit down!
Remove that bubblegum from your mouths
And please don't clown around!

He's coming with a clipboard.
That's not at all good news!
Be on your best behavior!
Don't act like little fools!

Turn the TV off; cut on the lights.
Drop everything and read.
At least look like you're reading.
It's good advice; take heed!

He's evaluating me, I'm sure.
That's what he's paid to do,
But boys and girls, remember,
I'm evaluating you!

Pencil and Eraser

"I don't need you to help me write,
To help me draw a plane or kite,
Or draw some gelatin or some snakes,
Or anything that slithers and shakes.
I can do without you," Pencil said,
"Because *my* body is made of lead."

"I see your point," Eraser said.
"It's true; your body *is* made of lead,
But do you think you can do without me?
Can you erase a *two* or the number *three*?
Can you erase a *T* or the letter *I*?
What about an *X* and the letter *Y*?
You make mistakes, and when you do,
I'm here to correct those mistakes for you.
I'm here to help you get them right.
Anytime—both day and night.
But if you think I'm a useless tool,
I'll hop off your head before you go to school.
Will you really get along without me?
Soon we shall see. Yes, we shall see."

Lorraine L. Hollowell

So Pencil went off to school that day
In a little boy's bookbag two miles away.
Eraser was missing from the top of its head.
Pencil thought it would do fine
'Cause that's what it said.

But instead of a Y, the little boy wrote T.
And instead of a two, the little boy wrote three.
"This pencil's no good!" the little boy said.
"The eraser is missing from the top of its head!"

Because this little boy hated making mistakes-
Mistakes that this pencil just could not erase,
Into the wastebasket, the pencil, he threw.
Then he reached in his desk and found one so new.

Pencil learned its lesson that day
When the little boy decided to throw it away.
Its biggest mistake was thinking its body of lead
Didn't need an eraser on top of its head.

My Pencil Had Control of Me

But teacher . . .
My pencil had control of me!
I tried to make it write a *three*.
Instead it wrote a *twenty-two*,
And it wrote *flu* instead of *flew*.
It wrote *Grant* instead of *Lee*.
It had control of me, you see?
It's taken over all day long.
That's why I got my answers wrong!

Where's Tim?

Tim went in the bathroom,
But he never *did* come out.
I sometimes wonder if he went
Up the water sprout.

The last thing we heard Tim say was:
"*I've got to use the john!*"
Then he rushed into the bathroom,
And now the poor boy's gone.

Miss Tereska had taught for an hour
When she noticed his empty seat.
She sent me in the bathroom
To take a little peek.

I went in there and looked around,
But I found no trace of Tim,
And to this very day no one
Has seen or heard from him.

Lorraine L. Hollowell

The Oatmeal Bath

Oatmeal Soap
Is my favorite kind.
It gets the deep down dirt.
It makes my toenails shine.

It makes me feel so clean;
It makes me feel brand new.
It makes my fat cheeks gleam
And my forehead too.

I really like this soap;
I use it every day.
It's the only soap
That keeps *my* dirt away.

I love the way it smells!
Adore the way it floats!
Yes, my favorite soap
Is *Oatmeal Soap!*

When I discovered that
I had not one bar more,
I rushed immediately
To *The Oatmeal Store.*

As I hurried along
From aisle to aisle,
I saw *Kvory, Strest,*
And a soap called *Trile.*

But *Oatmeal Soap*
I simply did not see
What was I to do?
Oh, mercy, mercy me!

Then I thought to myself,
"I think I'll hurry home
And make a bar of soap
Of my very own!"

I ran straight to the kitchen
When I got home,
And inside the cupboard,
I began to roam.

Lorraine L. Hollowell

I found a bag of sugar
And some sea salt too.
No cinnamon at all!
Ginger would have to do.

We had lots of oatmeal!
Eight boxes at least!
Was Mom preparing
For an oatmeal feast?

Next I went to the frig,
And took out the milk,
And two sticks of sweet butter
As smooth as pure silk.

Then I thought to myself,
"Why should I waste time?
A bar isn't necessary;
These ingredients are fine."

So into the tub,
I ran water, so hot,
And I added the ingredients
Right on the spot.

After dropping them all
Into the tub,
I hopped in too.
Then I started to scrub.

The Oatmeal Bath

But some of the oatmeal,
I accidently tasted,
And it tasted so good!
How on earth could waste it?!

So I ate and I ate.
Oh, my, it was yummy!
An oatmeal bath
Inside of my tummy!

Before long my bath
Was about half way finished.
Soon every bit of it
Would be diminished.

I continued eating.
I just couldn't stop
Until this yummy bath
Was eaten all up.

Oatmeal baths
Are so tasty and sweet!
Bet you anything
They beat *Cream of Wheat*!

Lorraine L. Hollowell

Don't Forget the Toilet Paper

Don't forget the toilet paper
When you're at the store.
Our last roll has been used up.
We're going to need some more.

We can do without the toothpaste
And even soap, I guess,
But if you forget the toilet paper,
We'll soon be in a mess.

If you forget the milk or bread,
I'm sure we'll be okay.
But, I need some toilet paper,
And I need it right away!

My Brother Drives a Car

My brother thinks he's really cool
'Cause he can drive a car.
But I don't think he's all that cool
'Cause he's never driven far.

Lorraine L. Hollowell

Strange Drivers

Russell drives his car in reverse,
But it couldn't be any worst
Than Skippy who drives with no steering wheel,
Or Jay who drives a yellow daffodil.

My Little Train

My little train is all run down.
I think that it is through.
Its little caboose has lost a wheel,
And its engine has lost two.

I want it to move around the track,
But it refuses to.
It's all pooped out; it's given up.
It just won't *choo, choo, choo.*

Failed Bank Robbery

He tried to rob a bank that day.
He really tried to get away,
But the robber's old getaway car
Didn't take him very far.

Upon the road came the robber's cat.
He swerved to miss it and got a flat.
The cops arrived . . .
And that was that.

Lorraine L. Hollowell

Max's Trampoline

Max got on his trampoline
And did a super flip.
He flipped right off that brand new thing
And landed on his hip.

Sure, Max was in a little pain,
But he crawled back on again.
He did another super flip
And landed on his chin.

He got back on a third time
And did four flips in a row!
But on the fourth flip, Max flipped off
And nearly broke a toe.

With much determination,
He got back on once more.
This time he did a super flip
That flipped him out the door.

He bumped his head; he bruised my back,
And even tore his spleen.
"That's it! No more!" Max shouted.
"This trampoline's too mean!"

Mr. and Mrs. McTony

Mr. and Mrs. McTony
Last night ate expired baloney.
Now they're in bed.
The two almost dead-
Should've eaten their fresh abalone.

The Secret

Joyce told me a secret today,
And her secret's safe with me.
I'm going to keep her secret
For all eternity!

If you don't believe me
Just ask Scott MaGee.
I shared her secret with him today
At a quarter and a half past three.

He promised to keep her secret,
And I know that Scott won't tell
'Cause Scott MaGree is just like me.
He keeps a secret well.

Lorraine L. Hollowell

Bud

I have a pet pig
Whose name is Bud.
He sleeps in a bed
But never in mud.

He eats at a table
And sits in a chair.
He brushes his teeth
And combs his short hair.

He uses soft tissue
When he blows his nose,
And he always blows gently
Whenever he blows.

When he's out in public,
He always wears clothes.
Bud's as human as I am,
As far as he knows.

You're Invited to My Party

You're invited to my party.
You, and all who read this line:
Come to my house Saturday morning
at an hour and a half past nine.

I live on M-Smith Road,
House Number Z-3 Four,
In Accomac, Virginia
On Virginia's Eastern Shore.

It's a birthday celebration
With friends, both old and new.
Oh, won't you please come join us,
If you've nothing else to do?

I doubt I've ever met you.
I might not know your name,
But I've decided to invite you.
Yes, I'll invite you just the same.

On the thirteenth of November
Is the celebration date.
I hope that you can make it,
And that you won't be late.

But there's something you must remember.
It is something you must do.
If you're coming to the party,
Be sure to bring a gift with you.

Lorraine L. Hollowell

Tommy Ball Walks on the Wall

Meet my best friend, Tommy Ball.
He walks like a spider on the wall.
He hangs from the ceiling like a spider too,
And he's not even using glue!

Where Invisible Creatures Play

I would like to go some day
Where all invisible creatures play.

They're sliding down an invisible slide
And behind invisible trees, they hide.

They're running here and running there
In their invisible underwear.

You can't see them jump and skip,
Nor can you see them do a flip.

But they're having such invisible fun-
Each and every invisible one.

Lorraine L. Hollowell